THE SCIENCE MUSEUM

the Moon

BSc PhD FBIS

LONDON HER MAJESTY'S STATIONERY OFFICE

Introduction

On 24 July 1969, the Apollo 11 capsule splashed down in the Pacific Ocean at the end of one of the most spectacular missions of exploration ever undertaken by man. Three American astronauts had just returned from a trip to the moon. Two of them, Neil Armstrong and Edwin Aldrin, had secured a place in history by becoming the first men to set foot on the dusty surface of the moon. Ten years before no one had reached more than 40 kilometres above the surface of the earth, and the best pictures of the moon could not distinguish objects less than 300 metres across. The exploits of the spacemen who conquered the 380,000 kilometres of space between us and the moon match those of the great explorers of the past. Their real life adventures rival those of fictional heroes like Dan Dare.

This booklet will tell the story of man's early ventures in space leading up to his first landing on the moon. It will discuss some of the problems facing the planners and designers during the early stages of the programme, for such an achievement depended on a support staff of millions. In a booklet of this length the story can be told only in general terms, and for more detailed descriptions the reader is referred to the short bibliography at the back.

The story of spaceflight can be traced back to the use of war rockets by the Chinese almost 1000 years ago and the ancestor of the modern space rocket, the German V2, made its appearance during World War 2. Our story however, will begin on 25 May 1961. On that day President Kennedy, influenced no doubt by a succession of Russian space 'firsts', said '. . . I believe that this nation should commit itself to achieving the goal, before this decade is out, of landing a man on the moon and returning him safely to the earth'. With this statement President Kennedy really began the 'moon race' and set in motion the most concentrated and sustained period of technological advance ever experienced in times of peace.

1 The German V2 rocket.

The problems

Before a man could land on the moon with any hope of a safe return there were many difficulties to be overcome. Very little was known about the moon's surface beyond what our telescopes could tell us. Some scientists believed that the moon was covered with a thick layer of dust that would engulf any landing spacecraft. The rockets available in 1961 were too small to carry a man and all his equipment to the moon, and were so unreliable that about half of them blew up at launch.

The astronaut would have to live in space for at least a week and carry with him all the air, water and food he needed for that time. He would have to withstand temperatures on the moon and in space which exceed 100°C in full sunlight but fall to −150°C in the shade.

The distances and speeds involved were immense. The distance to the moon is 380,000 kilometres, equivalent to ten times around the earth, and to escape the earth's gravitational field a rocket must accelerate to over 40,000km/hr which is twenty times Concorde's maximum cruising speed.

The next four sections describe how the major problems of learning more about the moon, providing reliable and powerful rockets, planning the voyage to the moon and keeping a man alive in space were overcome.

Unmanned exploration of the moon

The launch of Sputnik 1, the world's first artificial satellite, on 4 October 1957 took the world by surprise. This Russian achievement caused a flurry of activity in America, where it had been expected that the first man-made satellite to orbit the earth would be launched by her own Vanguard rocket. The signals from Sputnik 1 were picked up by receiving stations all over the world and announced to all that the 'space age' had begun.

Before long spacecraft from Russia and America were

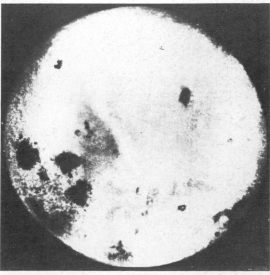

2 A model of Sputnik 1 – the world's first artificial satellite. Launched 4 October 1957.

3 Rear surface of the moon as photographed by Russia's Luna 3 on 6 October 1959.

(3)

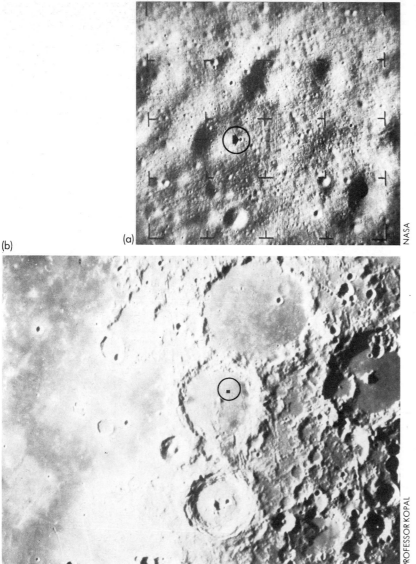

(b)

(a)

NASA

PROFESSOR KOPAL

4 The region of the moon near the Alphonsus crater as photographed by:

(a) Ranger 9 on 24 March 1965 from a height of 7 km. The small crater marked is 50 m across.

(b) A large earth-based telescope, the 108 cm reflector at Pic-du-Midi in the Pyrennees.
Note the far better resolution in the Ranger photograph. The square on photograph (b) shows the area covered by photograph (a).

aimed at the moon, our nearest neighbour in space. Many early launches failed, but by 1960 Russia's Luna 2 spacecraft had crashed into the moon and Luna 3 had photographed its rear surface. This gave man his first glimpse of the far side of the moon that always points away from us.

Such unmanned lunar probes were explorers in their own right, but they were also an essential preliminary to any manned exploration. Russia has not yet attempted to land a man on the moon and we cannot be sure that her Luna spacecraft were pathfinders for a future manned landing. However there is no doubt that the primary aim of America's three unmanned lunar programmes of the 1960s – Ranger, Surveyor and Orbiter – was to gather information for her manned moon landing programme. That programme was called Apollo.

Ranger

Nine spacecraft in the Ranger series were launched between 1961 and 1965. Ranger was designed to photograph the moon. Only three of the spacecraft operated as planned, but they sent back over 17,000 close-up pictures before crashing into the moon. Surface features only 30 centimetres across could be seen and, at the time, the pictures were described as providing the greatest single advance in lunar knowledge since Galileo and his telescope.

Orbiter

Five Orbiter spacecraft were launched in 1966 and 1967. All were successful. Their task was to photograph potential Apollo landing sites along the lunar equator. The first three spacecraft were so successful that Orbiters 4 and 5 were placed into an orbit passing over the moon's poles to obtain a photographic record of most of its surface.

Surveyor

Seven Surveyor spacecraft were launched between 1966 and 1968 to soft-land on the moon. Five were successful. They performed experiments on the strength, composition and structure of the surface, proving that the moon could withstand the weight of a manned lander. Some of the 80,000 pictures transmitted showed objects less than 1 centimetre across.

These programmes provided enough information about the moon to allow America to proceed with her plans to land a man there. There have been no unmanned American lunar missions since Surveyor 7 in January 1968. Meanwhile Russia's lunar exploration programme had run almost in parallel with America's, and it was her Luna 9 spacecraft that became the first man-made object to operate on the surface of the moon. Luna 9 soft-landed on 3 February 1966 and ejected a capsule 60 centimetres in diameter onto the surface. The panels of this capsule unfolded and it began transmitting the first picture taken on the moon. Russia's Luna spacecraft were also sent to crash into the moon on missions resembling those of Ranger, while others were placed in orbit around the moon. Luna 10 became the moon's first artificial satellite on 3 April 1966, stealing another space 'first' from under the nose of America's swiftly expanding space programme. Unlike the American Orbiter spacecraft however, Luna 10 carried no cameras to photograph the moon's surface.

Russia continued to explore the moon with unmanned probes even after the first men had landed. These spacecraft became more and more sophisticated and two of them in particular, Lunas 16 and 17, demonstrated how the moon could be explored efficiently and relatively cheaply using unmanned spacecraft.

Luna 16 soft-landed in the Sea of Fertility on 20 September 1970. It collected 100 grams of lunar soil and stored it inside a capsule mounted on top of the spacecraft. Next day this capsule with the samples hermetically sealed inside took off from the moon, using the descent stage as a launching platform, and brought them back safely to earth.

Two months later another event of considerable importance for robot exploration of the moon and the planets took place. On 17 November 1970 Luna 17 landed in the Sea of Rains and unloaded an eight-wheeled vehicle, Lunokhod 1. This was a mobile laboratory controlled by scientists in Russia. It roamed over the moon, taking readings during the lunar day and hibernating by night. Lunokhod 1 operated for nearly a year during which it covered an overall distance of 10 kilometres analysing the lunar soil and studying rocks and craters at several points on the way.

NASA

5

5 A spectacular view across the crater Copernicus taken by Orbiter 2 on 23 November 1966.

6 The Surveyor 3 spacecraft on the moon being inspected by the Apollo 12 astronaut Alan Bean.

NASA

6

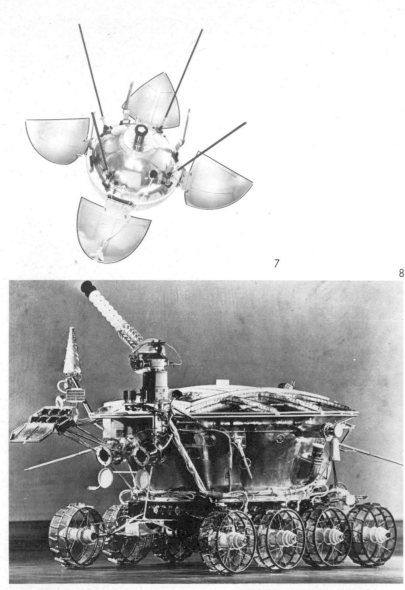

7

8

These two missions and their successful repeats (Luna 20 in February 1972 and Luna 21 carrying Lunokhod 2 in January 1973) resurrected the discussion on the relative merits of manned and unmanned explorers. Although Luna 16 brought back far less moon rock than Apollo 11 (100 grams compared with about 20 kilogrammes) and although Lunokhod 1 travelled a shorter distance over the moon than the later Apollo astronauts with their Lunar Rover, the importance of the Russian missions should not be overlooked. Flights like Luna 16 or Luna 17 can be undertaken at a fraction of the cost of an Apollo type mission and at no risk to human life; but there is no rigid answer to the question of whether manned or unmanned exploration is best. Each has its own merits and the two systems are complementary and not mutually exclusive.

In addition to her Luna programme, Russia also flew a series of large spacecraft, code named Zond, around the moon and back safely to earth between 1968 and 1970. Although these flights established Russia's capability to fly a man around the moon the programme was never taken to its logical conclusion. It is possible that problems were experienced with the reliability of the Proton rocket used to launch the Zond spacecraft which prevented it being used for a manned launch.

The unmanned lunar probes described in this section were true explorers in their own right, but their pioneering exploits have been lost in the glare of publicity that enveloped the manned missions to the moon.

The Launch Vehicles

The only type of vehicle at present capable of launching a satellite into orbit or sending a man to the moon is the rocket. To escape from earth's gravitational pull these rockets must accelerate to at least 40,000 km/hr.

To reach these speeds they must be extremely powerful and practical space rockets consume prodigious amounts of fuel. The first stage of the Saturn V rockets used to land the first men on the Moon burnt about 4000 gallons of propellent every second. In a typical rocket the fuel usually amounts to between 90 and 95 per cent of the take-off weight, whereas the spacecraft itself contributes

7 Model of the Luna 9 capsule – the first spacecraft to soft-land on the moon on 3 February 1966.

8 Lunokhod 1 – landed on the moon on 17 November 1970.

only 2 or 3 per cent. The difference is made up by the weight of the rocket. Before May 1961 the heaviest satellite launched by America was Midas 2, a military reconnaissance satellite. It weighed just over 2 tonnes. Russia's rockets of the early 1960s were far more powerful than America's and by 1961 she had placed satellites weighing over 7 tonnes into orbit. This launch capability, which accounts for Russia's early space successes, stems directly from the size of the nuclear bombs produced in the 1950s. Russia's nuclear warheads were heavier than the more sophisticated American ones and she had concentrated on the development of more powerful rockets to achieve the same range.

However by 1961 America had already begun developing a whole range of much more powerful rockets. In the context of the manned moon landing programme this work led to the Saturn family of which three types were produced, Saturn1, Saturn 1B and Saturn V. These were used for all the unmanned and manned Apollo missions.

The Saturn V rocket, used on all Apollo flights to the moon, is the biggest rocket ever built. It towers 110 metres above the ground, twice as high as Nelson's Column in Trafalgar Square, its maximum diameter is 10 metres and it weighs 3000 tonnes at launch. The five F1 engines used in the first stage develop a thrust of 33,400,000 newtons which is equivalent to the thrust of 160 Jumbo jet engines. An idea of the power difference between the Saturn V rockets and those of 1961 vintage can be gained from the fact that the escape tower – for use in the event of a launch failure – on Saturn V was more powerful than the actual Redstone rockets used to carry the first American 'astronauts' on sub-orbital hops in 1961. The smaller Saturn 1 and 1B rockets with thrusts of almost 7,000,000 newtons were used to test fly unmanned Apollo spacecraft and for manned Apollo missions that stayed in earth orbit.

Few details have been released of Russian rockets and launches. It was not until 1967, 6 years after the event, that the rocket used to launch the first man into space was shown in public. This Vostok rocket, 38 metres tall and with a first stage thrust of 5,000,000 newtons, was extremely powerful for its time and was only slightly smaller than Saturn 1. However, as noted earlier, it is more than probable that Russia experienced problems

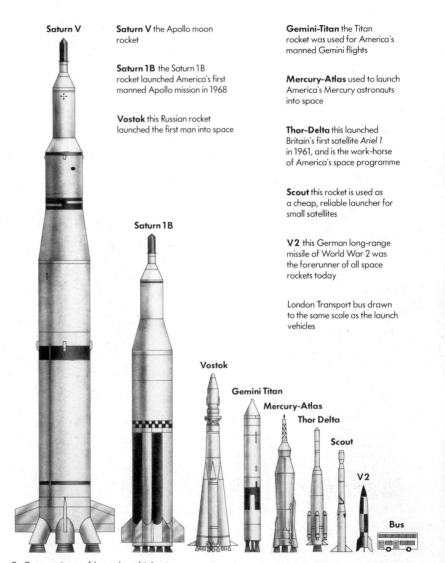

Saturn V

Saturn V the Apollo moon rocket

Saturn 1B the Saturn 1B rocket launched America's first manned Apollo mission in 1968

Vostok this Russian rocket launched the first man into space

Gemini-Titan the Titan rocket was used for America's manned Gemini flights

Mercury-Atlas used to launch America's Mercury astronauts into space

Thor-Delta this launched Britain's first satellite *Ariel 1* in 1961, and is the work-horse of America's space programme

Scout this rocket is used as a cheap, reliable launcher for small satellites

V2 this German long-range missile of World War 2 was the forerunner of all space rockets today

London Transport bus drawn to the same scale as the launch vehicles

Saturn 1B

Vostok

Gemini Titan

Mercury-Atlas

Thor Delta

Scout

V2

Bus

9 Comparison of launch vehicle sizes.

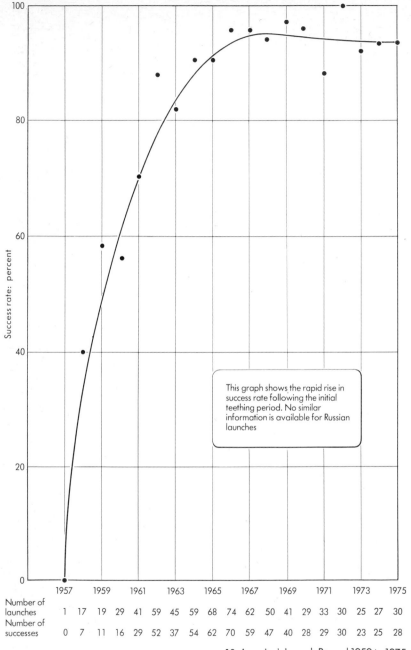

This graph shows the rapid rise in success rate following the initial teething period. No similar information is available for Russian launches

| Number of launches | 1 | 17 | 19 | 29 | 41 | 59 | 45 | 59 | 68 | 74 | 62 | 50 | 41 | 29 | 33 | 30 | 25 | 27 | 30 |
| Number of successes | 0 | 7 | 11 | 16 | 29 | 52 | 37 | 54 | 62 | 70 | 59 | 47 | 40 | 28 | 29 | 30 | 23 | 25 | 28 |

10 America's Launch Record 1959 to 1975.

with the development of rockets of the Saturn V class. This might have caused her to withdraw for the present any plans she may have had of putting a man on the moon. Another problem associated with the pre-1961 rockets was their reliability. For obvious reasons a rocket used to launch a man should be as reliable as possible and any launch failure was extremely undesirable from a purely financial point of view. At the time of President Kennedy's speech America's launch record left much to be desired and about half of her 75 satellite launchings had ended in disaster. German engineers had experienced the same problem of a high proportion of early failures in the development of their V2 rockets, and we have no reason to believe that the Russian space programme escaped its fair share. After 1961 America's success rate improved and the record of her Saturn rockets has been excellent with no real failures occurring in the 32 Saturn launches to date.

In the period of less than ten years from 1961 to 1969 America's space launch vehicles had grown from unreliable and relatively small rockets with thrusts of less than 500,000 newtons to massive, trouble-free goliaths with thrusts of 33,400,000 newtons capable of carrying payloads of 40 tonnes to the moon.

Flight plans

It is one thing to say that a man will land on the moon by a certain date, but quite another thing to decide how it will actually be done. Ideas had already appeared in 1960 for a spacecraft called Apollo to fly three men around the moon, but none of the practical details had been worked out. This circum-lunar Apollo spacecraft became the basis for the Apollo moon landing programme and, following President Kennedy's speech, the engineers began in earnest to consider the problems involved in taking a man to the moon. Three ways of sending a man to the moon were considered all through 1961 and up to July 1962 when the choice was made.

The Direct Ascent method

The simplest way of sending a man to the moon was the direct ascent method in which one large rocket would send the complete Apollo spacecraft to the moon. The whole spacecraft would land on the moon and, except for a lunar descent stage, would take off again at the end of the mission to return to earth.

At first this was the most favoured of the three methods. Its biggest disadvantage was the enormous rocket needed. The proposal called for a rocket 135 metres tall with a first stage thrust of 56 million newtons – nearly twice that of the Saturn V rocket finally used. Because the whole spacecraft had to land on the moon the astronauts mounted on top would be a long way from the surface. One proposal called for a lunar lander over 20 metres tall which could cause difficulty in seeing the surface during the critical landing phase, and might prevent the astronauts taking over manual control in an emergency to avoid boulders or craters as happened on Apollo 11.

The Earth Orbital Rendezvous method (EOR)

In this procedure two Saturn V class rockets, or several smaller ones, would carry pieces of the Apollo spacecraft into orbit around the earth where the spacecraft would be assembled. The completed spacecraft would be fired towards the moon and the mission would proceed as for Direct Ascent. This did not require such a large rocket as for Direct Ascent, but it still suffered from the problem of lack of visibility when landing. Rather more important was the fact that it required the successful launching of two or more rockets in quick succession, which was a daunting prospect in 1961, and it relied on the untried technique of rendezvous and docking of two spacecraft in orbit.

The Lunar Orbital Rendezvous method (LOR)

The third possible method was for one Saturn V class rocket to send the whole spacecraft to the moon and for a small lunar lander to descend to the surface leaving the rest of the spacecraft in lunar orbit. At the end of the stay on the moon the lander's ascent stage would rise and dock with the orbiting spacecraft. After the crew had transferred to the spacecraft for the journey home the lander would be jettisoned.

This method had the advantage that a purpose-built lunar lander could be used, thus overcoming the visi-

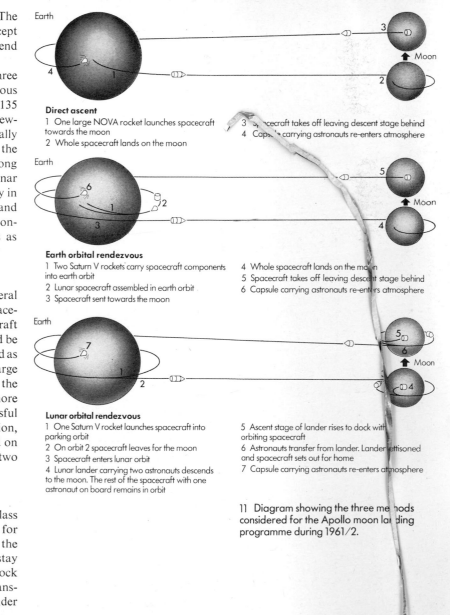

Direct ascent
1 One large NOVA rocket launches spacecraft towards the moon
2 Whole spacecraft lands on the moon
3 Spacecraft takes off leaving descent stage behind
4 Capsule carrying astronauts re-enters atmosphere

Earth orbital rendezvous
1 Two Saturn V rockets carry spacecraft components into earth orbit
2 Lunar spacecraft assembled in earth orbit
3 Spacecraft sent towards the moon
4 Whole spacecraft lands on the moon
5 Spacecraft takes off leaving descent stage behind
6 Capsule carrying astronauts re-enters atmosphere

Lunar orbital rendezvous
1 One Saturn V rocket launches spacecraft into parking orbit
2 On orbit 2 spacecraft leaves for the moon
3 Spacecraft enters lunar orbit
4 Lunar lander carrying two astronauts descends to the moon. The rest of the spacecraft with one astronaut on board remains in orbit
5 Ascent stage of lander rises to dock with orbiting spacecraft
6 Astronauts transfer from lander. Lander jettisoned and spacecraft sets out for home
7 Capsule carrying astronauts re-enters atmosphere

11 Diagram showing the three methods considered for the Apollo moon landing programme during 1961/2.

12 The Apollo 10 Command Module (CM).

13 Section of unused Apollo Heatshield.

bility problem, and the Saturn V rocket already under development would be powerful enough. However it relied on the completely untried process of docking, and this would have to be carried out not only near the earth but 380,000 kilometres away round the moon. The apparent dangers involved made this method unpopular at first.

After several changes of emphasis, NASA (the American National Aeronautics and Space Administration) announced in July 1962 that it had selected the LOR method for the Apollo manned moon landing programme. It was felt that the 'super' rocket needed for the simplest Direct Ascent approach would not be ready for a landing by 1970. Considerations of cost, chance of success and early completion all favoured the LOR method, and calculations had shown that it was at least as safe as the other methods.

Man in space

Space is a totally alien environment. An astronaut is connected to home and safety only by a tenuous radio link and his faith in the engineers who designed and built his spacecraft. During launch he must withstand the stresses (g-forces) caused by the rocket's acceleration. In space he is weightless – there is no up or down. Outside his spacecraft lies almost perfect vacuum. There is no air to breathe and nothing to protect him from the sun's blinding rays, from cosmic rays or the impact of small dust particles known as micrometeoroids. He experiences a wide range of temperatures.

To protect himself an astronaut carries his own habitable environment with him in his spacecraft and spacesuit.

The spacecraft

A typical spacecraft, such as the Apollo Command Module (CM) or Capsule, which houses the astronauts on their flights in space, consists of a pressurized inner container and an outer-shell which provides thermal insulation and protection against dust particle impact. The inner container holds the breathable atmosphere. In all American spacecraft before 1973 this was pure oxygen at one third atmospheric pressure but a normal mixture of oxygen and nitrogen at atmospheric pressure was used in Russian craft. America's Skylab spacecraft, where astronauts lived for up to three months, had an atmosphere of 75 per cent oxygen, 25 per cent nitrogen at one third atmospheric pressure. This was thought to be medically desirable and also to reduce the fire risk.

The reason for adopting a pressure well below normal atmospheric pressure in American craft is that the spacecraft does not need to be so strong, and can therefore be lighter. In the early stages of the manned space programme, Russia, with her more powerful launch vehicles, could beat the weight penalty but America could not. The cabins of these spacecraft were cramped. In the case of Apollo, which was relatively spacious, three men had to live for over a week in a volume about the same as that inside a medium-sized estate car.

The heatshield which protects the capsule from the intense heat developed on re-entry into the earth's atmosphere is part of the outer-shell. Temperatures as high as 2700°C are reached – cast iron melts at 1100°C. The Apollo heatshield is made by filling a honeycomb structure with a suitable material – an epoxy resin – that slowly vaporises at re-entry temperatures leaving the surface relatively cool. The heatshield on an Apollo capsule loses about a centimetre of material during re-entry.

The spacesuit

The suit is essentially a portable shelter which enables an astronaut to work outside his spacecraft. Sometimes, for example during launch, it is worn in a modified form inside the spacecraft for added safety. The basic Apollo suit has a cloth inner layer for comfort, a rubber-coated nylon bladder and an outer nylon restraint harness which aids mobility.

The basic Apollo suit is, however, never used on its own. When worn inside the spacecraft an extra three-layer garment is added to the basic suit which is then connected to the spacecraft's environmental system. A helmet, gloves and boots are clamped on.

When worn outside the spacecraft on Extra-Vehicular Activity (EVA) the suit takes over the thermal insulation and dust particle protection roles of the spacecraft. The astronaut wears an extra 17-layer garment over the basic

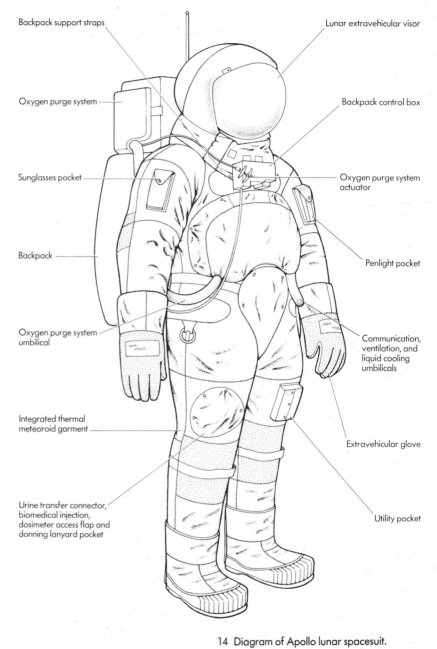

14 Diagram of Apollo lunar spacesuit.

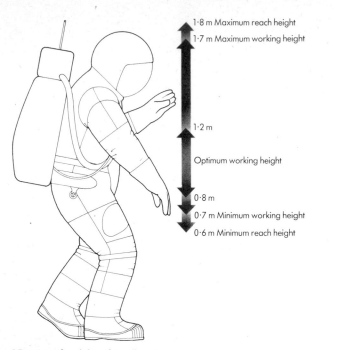

1·8 m Maximum reach height
1·7 m Maximum working height

1·2 m

Optimum working height

0·8 m
0·7 m Minimum working height
0·6 m Minimum reach height

15 Limits of mobility of Apollo astronauts on the moon's surface.

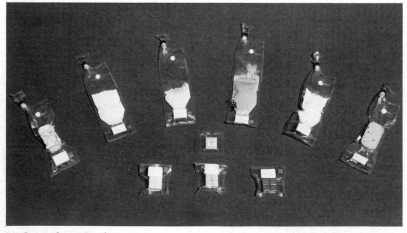

16 Gemini Space Food.

17 America's first spacewalk – Ed White outside Gemini 4 on 3 June 1965.

suit and a watercooled undergarment, which keeps the astronaut cool while working on the moon, replaces the 'long johns' normally worn beneath the basic suit. On the moon's surface, the astronaut's needs are supplied by a Portable Life Support System (PLSS) carried on his back. He wears an extra pair of insulated overboots and a darkened sun shield visor on the helmet to prevent him being blinded by the sun. The whole suit weighs 83 kilogrammes on earth, but this does not worry the astronauts on the moon where it only weighs 14 kilogrammes.

One problem in spacesuit design was to ensure that the astronauts could move around sufficiently freely. The Apollo astronauts' movements were quite limited and this was one reason why lunar samples were collected with tongs and scoops.

Medical problems

Before man had flown in space it was thought that his physical and mental capabilities might be affected by prolonged weightlessness, and that he might be subjected to dangerous levels of cosmic radiation. Yuri Gagarin's first spaceflight in April 1961 showed that man could live in space and, although this journey only lasted for 108 minutes, it gave encouragement to those interested in the future of manned spaceflight. In fact most of the early fears about man's health in space have proved groundless and, although several odd medical effects have been observed none have seriously affected man's ability for useful work. All astronauts undergo strenuous training to prepare them for the experience of spaceflight but, despite this, most astronauts suffer from space sickness early in their flights. This effect, similar to sea sickness, soon wears off, and there appears to be no medical reason why man cannot live in space for long periods of time. A constant check is kept on the health of all astronauts during their mission. Small medical detectors which monitor their heartbeats, pulse rates, breathing and temperature, are taped to their bodies.

Space food

All food eaten in space so far was prepared on earth. The alternative possibilities of regenerating food from waste products or growing it in space have received little serious consideration. The first space foods were simply

1

18 Apollo 9 – Astronaut Dave Scott leaves the Apollo command module.

19 The Launch of Apollo 11.

20 Edwin Aldrin descending the steps of the Apollo 11 Lunar Lander.

21 Edwin Aldrin standing on the moon's surface.

on following page
22 Apollo 15 astronaut James Irwin beside the lunar rover. Mount Hadley is in the background.

20

21

(15)

baby foods. Gemini and early Apollo astronauts ate dehydrated natural foods in bite-sized cubes or in a form that could be mixed with cold water and squeezed into the mouth. The cubes had an edible coating to prevent the formation of crumbs, and their corners were rounded to prevent cutting the astronauts' mouths. Later Apollo astronauts ate 'sticky' foods with a spoon and hot as well as cold water was available for reconstituting the dehydrated meals. These two factors made eating in space much more pleasant.

Early manned spaceflights

Man's first flight into space took place on 12 April 1961, only 3½ years after the launch of Sputnik 1. The Russian Yuri Gagarin made one orbit of the earth in his Vostok spacecraft. This 40,000 kilometre flight lasted for 108 minutes in contrast to the first trip around the world by Magellan's crew in 1519 which took 3 years. During the flight Gagarin rode in the 2·3 metre diameter, 2·4 tonne spherical re-entry capsule at the front of Vostok 1 which landed in Russia at the end of the mission. This flight, no less than that of Sputnik 1, spurred the space programme in America and led to President Kennedy's statement in May 1961.

The escape by man from the grip of earth's gravity was an event as significant as the first powered flight of the Wright brothers nearly sixty years before.

Further manned flights quickly followed Vostok 1, with Russian Vostok cosmonauts and American Mercury astronauts gaining spaceflight experience on longer and longer missions. Multi-crewed missions followed these one man flights. America's Gemini carried a crew of two, but three men were squeezed into Russia's Voskhod 1, which was a modified Vostok.

Events moved swiftly. In 1965 one Russian and two Americans walked in space. Russia's Alexi Leonov spent twenty minutes outside Voskhod 2 in March 1965, and the following June America's Ed White left his Gemini 4 spacecraft for a 21 minute walk in space. The pictures of White's walk brought the beauty of space into the homes of earthbound humans. Late in 1965 Gemini 6 and Gemini 7 made a rendezvous in orbit and

23 Major Yuri Gagarin (1934-1968) – the world's first spaceman.

24 Model of Vostok 1 – the world's first spaceship.

22

25   The Apollo 11 Astronauts

from left to right.

N Armstrong – Apollo 11 Commander.
The first man to walk on the moon. Now a
Professor at Cincinnati University.

M Collins – Apollo 11 Command Module
Pilot. Stayed in Lunar Orbit while Armstrong
and Aldrin landed on moon. Now Director
of National Air and Space Museum,
Smithsonian Institution, Washington.

E Aldrin – Apollo 11 Lunar Module Pilot.
The second man to walk on the moon. Now
a Consultant in California.

early in 1966 Gemini 8 successfully docked with an unmanned target vehicle. This was the first docking in space, an exercise vital for the manned moon landing programme.

Then, disaster struck both space programmes.

On 27 January 1967, fire, fed by the pure oxygen atmosphere, swept through the cabin of an Apollo capsule during a routine ground test. Three astronauts, Ed White, Virgil Grissom and Roger Chaffee died in the inferno.

On 24 April 1967 the first manned flight of Russia's latest spacecraft, Soyuz 1, was ended early because it was tumbling in orbit. The braking parachutes failed to deploy and the cosmonaut, Vladimir Komarov, died in the resulting crash. These tragedies were the subjects of long and careful investigations, and no further manned spaceflights took place for 18 months.

Then with time running out, if her goal of landing a man on the moon before 1970 was to be achieved, America launched her first manned Apollo mission in October 1968. The success of Apollo 7 went a long way towards healing the wound caused by the fire of 1967. Russia resumed her manned flights in 1968 but her interest in landing a man on the moon seemed to have evaporated – if it ever existed. America's build-up to a manned landing proceeded smoothly and swiftly. Apollo 8 carried the first men around the moon over Christmas 1968, Apollo 9 tested the moon landing system in earth orbit in March 1969 and Apollo 10 tested the complete system around the moon during May 1969 in a final, successful rehearsal.

The way was now clear for the main event of the American manned spaceflight programme – the landing of two men on the moon by Apollo 11.

The flight of Apollo 11

Just two months after Apollo 10, all was ready for the start of the most ambitious voyage of Exploration ever undertaken by man. After being confined to the earth for 3,000,000 years man was about to land on that symbol of unattainability – the moon. No longer could the phrase 'to reach for the moon' be used logically to mean attempting the impossible.

The Apollo spacecraft that carried the three Apollo 11 astronauts on this journey consisted of three main sections. The Service Module (SM) contained the engines used to manoeuvre in space and much of the equipment needed for the mission, eg fuel cells to provide electrical power. The Command Module (CM), or capsule, was the astronauts' home for most of the mission and was the only part of the spacecraft that returned safely to earth. The combined Command Module and Service Module were known by the acronym CSM. The Lunar Module (LM) was the spider-like spacecraft that carried two astronauts down to the surface of the moon. At the end of the stay its ascent stage lifted off and rose to dock with the rest of the spacecraft in lunar orbit.

16 July 1969   1332 hours GMT

The Saturn V rocket carrying the Apollo 11 spacecraft and astronauts Neil Armstrong, Edwin Aldrin and Michael Collins lifted off from Cape Kennedy (now known by its original name of Cape Canaveral) in Florida. Over 1,000,000 people saw the launch from Florida and another 500,000,000 watched it live on television screens all over the world. The pictures were transmitted via the INTELSAT communications satellites.

Twelve minutes later the spacecraft went into orbit around the earth.

16 July 1969   1616 hours GMT

On the second orbit the Saturn V rocket's third stage engine was refired to set Apollo 11 on course for the moon. The Apollo CSM separated from the third stage, turned through 180° and docked with the LM stored in the rocket. The complete spacecraft pulled clear of the spent rocket and continued on its way to the moon.

19 July 1969   1713 hours GMT

Three days later after an uneventful journey, Apollo 11 disappeared behind the moon. The SM engine was fired and the spacecraft entered lunar orbit.

20 July 1969   1747 hours GMT

The LM, code-named Eagle, with astronauts Armstrong and Aldrin on board separated from the CSM and began its descent towards the lunar surface. Collins remained

NASA

26 Tranquillity Base – man's first moon base.

27 The Apollo Lunar Spacecraft.

Service Module (SM)
height 7·5 m
maximum diameter 3·9 m
weight (fully loaded) 23·5 tonnes

Command Module (CM)
height 3·5 m
maximum diameter 3·9 m
weight (fully loaded) 5·5 tonnes

Lunar Module
height 7·0 m
maximum width (across legs) 9·5 m
weight (fully loaded) 15·2 tonnes

in the CSM, code-named Columbia, and as it passed behind the moon he must have felt that he was the loneliest man since Adam.

20 July 1969   2017 hours GMT

Eagle landed in the Sea of Tranquillity some 6 kilometres from the nominal landing site after Armstrong had manoeuvred Eagle to avoid landing in a large crater. The first man had arrived on the moon.

21 July 1969   0256 hours GMT

Neil Armstrong stepped off the bottom rung of Eagle's ladder. With the words 'That's one small step for a man, one vast leap for mankind', he became the first man to stand on the surface of the moon. One of Armstrong's first tasks was to collect a small contingency sample of lunar soil before he helped Aldrin down the ladder to join him.

On the first EVA on the moon, which lasted for nearly three hours, the astronauts stayed within thirty metres of the lunar lander. They practised walking on the moon with the characteristic 'kangaroo hops', collected more lunar rock samples, took many pictures of Tranquillity Base and performed in several publicity ceremonies. On the scientific side they set up two experiments, a moonquake detector and laser reflector. These would continue to operate long after the astronauts had departed. An aluminium foil detector was also placed on the moon to trap particles in the solar wind, a stream of mainly hydrogen nuclei blown out from the sun. This detector was brought back to earth for analysis.

At the end of the EVA the two astronauts brushed the lunar dust from their spacesuits before re-entering Eagle. Once inside they threw their PLSS, overshoes and cameras overboard in order to keep the contamination of the lunar module to a minimum.

21 July 1969   1754 hours GMT

Eagle's ascent rocket was fired and, using the descent stage as a launching platform, the ascent stage rose from the moon carrying Armstrong and Aldrin back into lunar orbit.

21 July 1969   2135 hours GMT

28
29

The ascent stage of Eagle docked with Columbia and Armstrong and Aldrin rejoined Collins in the cabin of Apollo 11. After jettisoning the LM, Columbia's engine was fired, and the astronauts started their journey home.

24 July 1969   1620 hours GMT

Just before reaching the top of the earth's atmosphere at the end of a return journey as uneventful as the outward stage, the CM was detached from the SM. The astronauts manoeuvred the re-entry capsule so that its blunt heat-shield faced forward in the direction of flight.

24 July 1969   1650 hours GMT

The Apollo 11 capsule splashed down in the Pacific Ocean about 21 km from the main recovery vessel, the USS *Hornet*.

The Apollo 11 mission was over. The astronauts, exhausted but fit, were handed Biological Isolation Garments before they left their capsule. These they put on before they were flown by helicopter to the USS *Hornet*. Immediately on arrival they were transferred to a Mobile Quarantine Facility (MQF), basically an isolation ward, where their health could be monitored without exposure to the outside environment. At the time it was thought possible that the astronauts might bring back some 'space bugs' with them.

On 27 July 1969 the USS *Hornet* reached Hawaii where the MQF, with the three astronauts still on board, was unloaded and flown to Houston. There the astronauts entered more spacious accommodation at the Lunar Receiving Laboratory for the remainder of their quarantine period. Meanwhile work had already begun on the study of the 21·8 kg of lunar samples they had brought back.

The astronauts were released from quarantine on 10 August 1969. They then began what must have been for them an even more nerve-racking experience than their recent spaceflight, a tour of American and then foreign cities, where they were fêted as modern-day heroes.

NASA

30

28 Edwin Aldrin erecting the Apollo 11 solar wind experiment.

29 President Nixon talking to the Apollo 11 astronauts through the window of the Mobile Quarantine Facility.

30 Eagle's ascent stage rises to dock with Columbia.

31 The Apollo 17 capsule splashes down in the Pacific Ocean on 19 December 1972 at the end of the last Apollo mission to the moon.

Conclusion

The success and apparent ease with which the Apollo 11 mission proceeded made the later Apollo missions appear something of an anti-climax in the eyes of the news media and the general public.

Six more manned missions to the moon followed Apollo 11. All except the ill-fated Apollo 13 were completely successful and the scientific content increased with each mission. The number of experiments performed on the moon and during the flights increased, the experimental packages (ALSEP) left behind became more sophisticated and heavier samples of moon rock were collected. The astronauts spent longer working on the moon's surface and travelled further from their base. On Apollos 15, 16 and 17 a lunar rover was used to carry the astronauts many kilometres across the moon.

Those who consider that the Apollo missions were simply expensive propaganda exercises underestimate the invaluable scientific work carried out. Work which because of its specialised nature rarely hits the headlines.

The last Apollo moon landing took place in 1972. Since then American astronauts have lived in space for up to 84 days in their Skylab space station, and Russia has carried out similar missions with her Salyut space stations.

But *What of the future?* There can be no doubt that man will continue to fly in space.

The American re-useable Space Shuttle launcher, being developed by NASA, will make space travel less prohibitively expensive. This aircraft-like space vehicle, which is scheduled to make its first flight in 1979, will return to earth to be used again at the end of each mission.

Looking into the crystal ball, one can foresee:

Permanent manned space stations in orbit around the earth.

A permanent laboratory and observatory on the moon.

A manned mission to Mars.

It is impossible to put a timescale on these events, and their cost might mean that they will have to await the arrival of a collaborative world space programme.

32 Permanent manned space station in earth orbit – artist's impression.

33 The Space Shuttle.

34 Manned observatory on the moon – artist's impression.

35 Manned Mars Lander – artist's impression.

Unmanned flights to the Moon

Spacecraft	Country	Launch Date	Comments
Project-Able 1	America	17.8.58	First known attempt to fly a spacecraft to the moon. Launch failure.
Pioneer 1	America	11.10.58	Failure.
Pioneer 2	America	8.11.58	Failure.
Pioneer 3	America	6.12.58	Failure.
Luna 1 (Lunik)	Russia	2.1.59	Flew past the moon. Nearest approach 6000km.
Pioneer 4	America	3.3.59	Flew past the moon. Nearest approach 60000km.
Luna 2	Russia	12.9.59	Became the first man-made object on the moon when it crashed into the Mare Imbrium on 13.9.59.
Luna 3	Russia	4.10.59	Flew behind the moon and transmitted the first pictures of the moon's hidden face.
Atlas-Able 4	America	26.11.59	Launch failure.
Atlas-Able 5A	America	25.9.60	Launch failure.
Atlas-Able 5B	America	15.12.60	Launch failure.
Ranger 1	America	23.8.61	Test launch for the Ranger programme. Partial success.
Ranger 2	America	18.11.61	As Ranger 1.
Ranger 3	America	26.1.62	First operational Ranger. Missed the moon.
Ranger 4	America	23.4.62	Failure.
Ranger 5	America	18.10.62	Failure.
Luna 4	Russia	2.4.63	Possible soft-landing attempt. Missed the moon.
Ranger 6	America	30.1.64	Crashed into the moon. Camera failure prevented pictures being taken.
Ranger 7	America	28.7.64	First successful Ranger mission. 4000 pictures returned.
Ranger 8	America	17.2.65	Success. 7000 pictures returned.
Ranger 9	America	21.3.65	Success. Transmitted live TV pictures.
Luna 5	Russia	9.5.65	Attempted soft-landing. Crashed into the moon.
Luna 6	Russia	8.6.65	Attempted soft-landing.
Zond 3	Russia	18.7.65	Photographed the moon on a bypass flight.
Luna 7	Russia	4.10.65	Attempted soft-landing.
Luna 8	Russia	3.12.65	Attempted soft-landing.
Luna 9	Russia	31.1.66	Soft-landed in the Sea of Storms. The first man-made object to operate on another heavenly body.
Luna 10	Russia	31.3.66	Entered lunar orbit to become the moon's first artificial satellite.
Surveyor 1	America	30.5.66	Successful soft-landing.
Orbiter 1	America	10.8.66	Photographed a 4800km strip of the lunar equator.
Luna 11	Russia	24.8.66	Entered lunar orbit.
Surveyor 2	America	20.9.66	Crashed into the moon.
Luna 12	Russia	22.10.66	Entered lunar orbit.
Orbiter 2	America	6.11.66	Success.
Luna 13	Russia	21.12.66	Soft-landed on the moon.
Orbiter 3	America	4.2.67	Completed the main task of the Orbiter series.
Surveyor 3	America	17.4.67	Mission successful despite a hard landing.
Orbiter 4	America	4.5.67	Entered a polar orbit around the moon. Obtained pictures of over 90% of the moon's surface.
Surveyor 4	America	14.7.67	Failure.
Orbiter 5	America	1.8.67	Successful repeat of Orbiter 4 mission.
Surveyor 5	America	8.9.67	Success.
Surveyor 6	America	7.11.67	Success. Made an 8·5 sec flight from the surface of the moon.
Surveyor 7	America	7.1.68	Success.
Zond 4	Russia	2.3.68	Possible attempted lunar fly around.
Luna 14	Russia	7.4.68	Entered lunar orbit.
Zond 5	Russia	15.9.68	Flew around the moon and returned to earth.
Zond 6	Russia	10.11.68	Successful repeat of Zond 5 mission.
Luna 15	Russia	13.7.69	Possible attempt to return lunar samples before Apollo 11.
Zond 7	Russia	8.8.69	Repeat of Zond 5 mission. Success.
Luna 16	Russia	12.9.70	Collected 100g of lunar soil and brought it back to earth.
Zond 8	Russia	20.10.70	Repeat of Zond 5.

Spacecraft	Country	Launch Date	Comments
Luna 17	Russia	10.11.70	Successfully unloaded a remotely controlled vehicle – Lunokhod 1 – onto the moon.
Luna 18	Russia	2.9.71	Crashed into the moon.
Luna 19	Russia	28.9.71	Entered lunar orbit.
Luna 20	Russia	14.2.72	Successful repeat of Luna 16 mission.
Luna 21	Russia	8.1.73	Released Lunokhod 2 onto the moon.
Luna 22	Russia	29.5.74	Entered lunar orbit.
Luna 23	Russia	28.10.74	Entered lunar orbit.
Luna 24	Russia	9.8.76	Repeat of Luna 16 mission.

Manned spaceflights

Spacecraft	Country	Astronaut/Cosmonaut	Launch Date	Flight Duration in hours	Comments
Vostok 1	Russia	Y Gagarin	12.4.61	1·8	Man's first spaceflight.
Mercury MR3	America	A Shepard	5.5.61	0·25	Sub-orbital hops not true spaceflights.
Mercury MR4	America	V Grissom	21.7.61	0·25	
Vostok 2	Russia	G Titov	6.8.61	25·3	
Mercury MA6	America	J Glenn	20.2.62	4·9	First American in space.
Mercury MA7	America	S Carpenter	24.5.62	4·9	
Vostok 3	Russia	A Nikolayev	11.8.62	94·4	Record stay in space.
Vostok 4	Russia	P Popovich	12.8.62	71·0	
Mercury MA8	America	W Schirra	3.10.62	9·2	
Mercury MA9	America	L Cooper	15.5.63	34·3	Completion of America's Mercury programme.
Vostok 5	Russia	V Bykovsky	14.6.63	119·1	Record stay in space.
Vostok 6	Russia	V Tereshkova	16.6.63	70·8	First woman in space.
Voskhod 1	Russia	V Komarov K Feokistov B Yegorov	12.10.64	24·3	First multi-crewed spaceflight.
Voskhod 2	Russia	A Leonov P Belyayev	18.3.65	26·0	World's first spacewalk by A Leonov (20 min).
Gemini 3	America	V Grissom J Young	23.3.65	4·9	America's first multi-crewed spaceflight.
Gemini 4	America	E White J McDivitt	3.6.65	97·9	America's first space walk by E White.
Gemini 5	America	L Cooper C Conrad	21.8.65	190·9	Record stay in space.

Spacecraft	Country	Astronaut/Cosmonaut	Launch Date	Flight Duration in hours	Comments
Gemini 7	America	F Borman J Lovell	4.12.65	330·6	Record stay in space.
Gemini 6	America	W Schirra T Stafford	15.12.65	25·9	Rendezvoused to within 30cm of Gemini 7.
Gemini 8	America	N Armstrong D Scott	16.3.66	10·7	First successful docking in space.
Gemini 9	America	T Stafford E Cernan	3.6.66	73·3	
Gemini 10	America	J Young M Collins	18.7.66	70·8	
Gemini 11	America	C Conrad R Gordon	12.9.66	71·3	
Gemini 12	America	J Lovell E Aldrin	11.11.66	94·6	
Soyuz 1	Russia	V Komarov	23.4.67	26·8	First fatality during a spaceflight. Spacecraft crashed on landing.
Apollo 7	America	W Schirra W Cunningham D Eisele	11.10.68	260·1	First manned flight of Apollo spacecraft.
Soyuz 3	Russia	G Beregovoy	26.10.68	94·9	Manoeuvred to within 200m of the unmanned Soyuz 2.
Apollo 8	America	F Borman J Lovell W Anders	21.12.68	147·0	First manned flight around the moon.
Soyuz 4	Russia	V Shatalov	14.1.69	71·2	Soyuz 4 docked with Soyuz 5. Khrunov and Yeliseyev transfer to Soyuz 4.
Soyuz 5	Russia	Y Khrunov B Volynov A Yeliseyev	15.1.69	72·8	
Apollo 9	America	J McDivitt D Scott R Schweickart	3.3.69	241·9	Tested complete Apollo spacecraft in earth orbit.
Apollo 10	America	T Stafford J Young E Cernan	18.5.69	192·1	Dress rehearsal for Apollo moon landing.
Apollo 11	America	N Armstrong E Aldrin M Collins	16.7.69	195·3	First manned landing on the moon. N Armstrong makes the first step.
Soyuz 6	Russia	G Shonin V Kubasov	11.10.69	118·4	
Soyuz 7	Russia	A Filipchenko V Volkov V Gorbatko	12.10.69	118·7	

Spacecraft	Country	Astronaut/ Cosmonaut	Launch Date	Flight Duration in hours	Comments
Soyuz 8	Russia	V Shatalov A Yeliseyev	13.10.69	118·8	
Apollo 12	America	C Conrad A Bean R Gordon	14.11.69	244·6	Second manned moon landing.
Apollo 13	America	J Lovell F Haise J Swigert	11.4.70	142·8	Moon landing aborted following explosion in Apollo service module.
Soyuz 9	Russia	A Nikolayev V Sevastyanov	1.6.70	425·0	Space duration record.
Apollo 14	America	A Shepard E Mitchell S Roosa	31.1.71	216·0	Third manned moon landing.
Soyuz 10	Russia	V Shatalov A Yeliseyev N Rukavishnikov	23.4.71	47·8	Docked with Salyut 1 space station.
Soyuz 11	Russia	G Dobrovolsky V Volkov V Patseyev	6.6.71	570·4	Docked and worked in Salyut space station. All three astronauts killed during re-entry. Space duration record.
Apollo 15	America	A Scott A Worden J Irwin	26.7.71	295·2	
Apollo 16	America	J Young T Mattingly C Duke	16.4.72	265·8	
Apollo 17	America	E Cernan R Evans H Schmitt	7.12.72	301·8	Completion of Apollo manned moon landing programme.
Skylab 2	America	C Conrad J Kerwin P Weitz	25.5.73	672·8	First crew to inhabit Skylab space station. Record stay in space.
Skylab 3	America	A Bean J Lousma O Garriott	28.7.73	1427·2	Record stay in space.
Soyuz 12	Russia	V Lazarev O Makarov	27.9.73	47·3	First Russian manned spaceflight since Soyuz 11.
Skylab 4	America	G Carr E Gibson W Pogue	16.11.73	2017·3	Record stay in space.
Soyuz 13	Russia	P Klimuk V Lebedev	18.12.73	188·9	

Spacecraft	Country	Astronaut/ Cosmonaut	Launch Date	Flight Duration in hours	Comments
Soyuz 14	Russia	P Popovich Y Artyukhin	3.7.74	378·5	Enter Salyut 3 space station.
Soyuz 15	Russia	G Sarafanov L Demin	26.8.74	48·2	Did not dock with Salyut 3.
Soyuz 16	Russia	A Filipchenko N Rukavishnikov	2.12.74	142·4	
Soyuz 17	Russia	A Gubarev G Grechko	11.1.75	708·5	First visit to Salyut 4 space station.
Soyuz 18	Russia	P Klimuk V Sevastynov	24.5.75	1511·3	Visited Salyut 4.
Soyuz 19	Russia	A Leonov V Kubasov	15.7.75	142·5	Joint American/Russian space mission. The two spacecraft dock in space.
Apollo 18	America	T Stafford D Slayton V Brand	15.7.75	216·5	
Soyuz 21	Russia	B Volynov V Zhdobov	6.7.76	1182·4	Docks with Salyut 5. Soyuz 20 was unmanned.
Soyuz 22	Russia	V Bykovsky V Aksenov	15.9.76	190·0	

Further reading

1 *Rockets, Missiles and Space Flight* W Ley, published by Chapman and Hall. 1951
This book provides a good introduction to the history of rocketry up to the early 1950s.
Although out of print, copies can be found in many second-hand book shops and most libraries.

2 *Journey to Tranquillity* H Young, B Silcock and P Dunn, published by Jonathon Cape, 1969
The background to the Apollo programme and the flight of Apollo 11 is described in this book.

3 *Apollo Expeditions to the Moon* edited by E Cortright NASA SP-350, 1976
This excellent book produced by NASA and sold only by the US Government Printing Office, Washington might be hard to obtain but it is well worth the effort. It consists of a collection of articles written by men actively involved with America's space programmes and is lavishly illustrated.

4 *The Frontiers of Space* by P Bono and K Gatland, 1971
Robot Explorers by K Gatland, 1972
Manned Spacecraft by K Gatland, 1971.
Missiles and Rockets by K Gatland, 1975

All published by Blandford.

This series of relatively cheap publications provides a good insight into all aspects of space travel.

Printed in England for Her Majesty's Stationery Office by Raithby, Lawrence & Company Limited at the De Montfort Press: Leicester and London
Dd 587504   K280   8/77